TREASURY OF LITERATURE

WRITER'S JOURNAL

D1383863

WHISPER A SONG

JUMP RIGHT IN

COLOR THE SKY

HARCOURT BRACE & COMPANY
Orlando Atlanta Austin Boston San Francisco Chicago Dallas New York
Toronto London

Grateful acknowledgment is made to Doubleday, a division of Bantam Doubleday Dell Publishing
Group, Inc. for permission to reprint "The Lamb" from *The Collected Poems of Theodore Roethke* by
Theodore Roethke.

Printed in the United States of America

ISBN 0-15-301267-6

5 6 7 8 9 10   030   97   96

Whisper
a
Song

CONTENTS
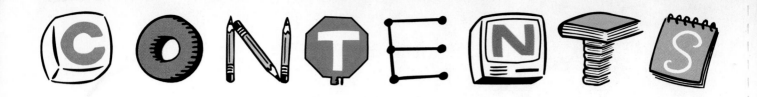

1

JUST·LIKE·ME

3–4

2

ALONG·THE·WAY

15–16

I Learn From My Friends

_____
(your name)

☞ Have children write about something they learned from a friend. Have them illustrate their work.

horse

lion

skates

dinosaur

ring

ball

baby doll

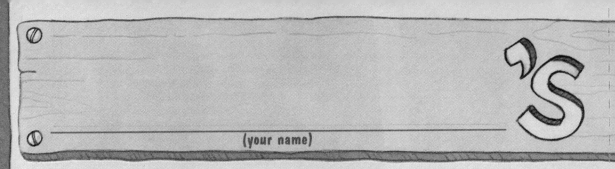

_____
_____
(your name)

's

 Have children imagine they are owners of toy shops. Ask them to draw the toys they will sell. Remind them that toy stores carry more than one of each item. Then have them list the toys, including the number of each that they will have on their shelves. (Example: "6 fire trucks")

My Toys

duck

robot

car

rag doll

bear

fire truck

jump rope

I KNOW ABOUT A RAINBOW

by

_____

(your name)

☞ Have children imagine that they are the child in the picture.
Have them write how a rainbow appeared in their mind.

Did you see what Yankee Doodle saw

"Along the Way"?

Turn to page 16.

Yankee Doodle Dandy

Yankee Doodle went to town,
riding on a pony,
Stuck a feather in his hat
and called it macaroni.

Along The Way

by _____
(your name)

Have children imagine they are walking through the town. Have them circle the things they like and add to the picture. On another sheet of paper, have children write about the things they see along the way.

My Silly Sally...

by _____
(your name)

☞ Have children draw a silly way that Silly Sally could go to town.
Ask them to write a sentence about their picture.

What will May do?

☞ Have children draw and write about what the characters are likely to do next.

What They Will Do

What will Juan do?

How _____ Likes to Move
(Your Name)

☞ Have children draw themselves moving in a way they enjoy. Have them write about what they are doing.

Where I Walked

by _____
(your name)

 Have children draw a line through the park showing where they would like to walk. Then have them list what they would see.

TEAR IT OUT

24

JUMP RIGHT IN

CONTENTS

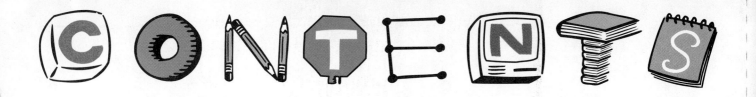

1 GIVE·IT·A·TRY
3–4

2 ON·OUR·OWN
13–14

Writer's Handbook   **H1–H6**

Give It a Try

Turn to page 4.

An eensy, weensy spider climbed
up the water spout,
Down came the rain and
washed the spider out.
Out came the sun and
dried up all the rain
And the eensy, weensy spider
climbed up the spout again.

_____
(your name)

Tries Something New

Have children circle the activities they have tried. Then have them write about something new they have tried.

's Favorite Game

_____
(your name)

Have children draw themselves telling the animals about their favorite game. Have them write what they would say in the word bubble and draw any game equipment they would need.

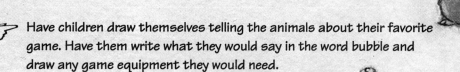

Can the cat see the duck?

_____ 's Clue
(your name)

Have children look at the picture. Then have them write a sentence that gives a clue about where the duck is hiding.

Find _____

(your name)

Look

Look
What do you see?
Me!

☞ Have children draw themselves hiding in the scene.
Then have them write where to look to find them, to
complete the poem.

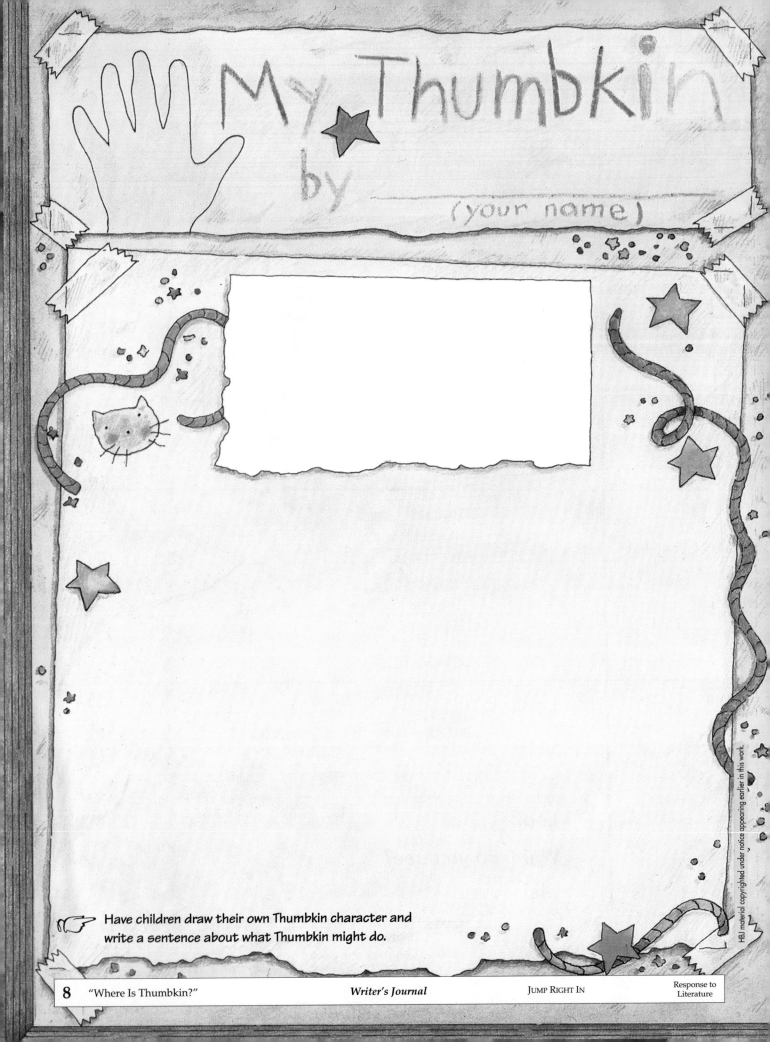

My ★ Thumbkin

by _____
(your name)

Have children draw their own Thumbkin character and write a sentence about what Thumbkin might do.

_____
(your name)

Hello, Turtle!

☞ Have children draw themselves beneath the word balloon. Then have them write a wish they might tell Turtle.

What Is Happening?

by _____

(your name)

Have children write a sentence about the main idea for each picture on page 10. Then have them draw their own picture and write a main idea sentence for it on page 11.

My Ride on the Wind

by _____
(your name)

I will *go*

👉 Have children draw a picture and write a sentence telling where they would go if they could ride on the wind.

On Our Own

Turn to page 14.

The Lamb just says, I AM!

He frisks and whisks, <u>He</u> can.

He jumps all *over*. Who

Are <u>you</u>? You're jumping too!

Theodore Roethke

_____ 's Bird

(Your Name)

☞ Have children complete the bird's nest and draw
a bird in it. Have them write what the bird might
say about its new home.

_____ Helps the Baby
(your name)

☞ Have children draw themselves doing something a baby cannot do. Have them write what they might tell the baby.

_____ **'s Things To Do**

(your name)

Have children write a sequenced list of things they might do in a day.

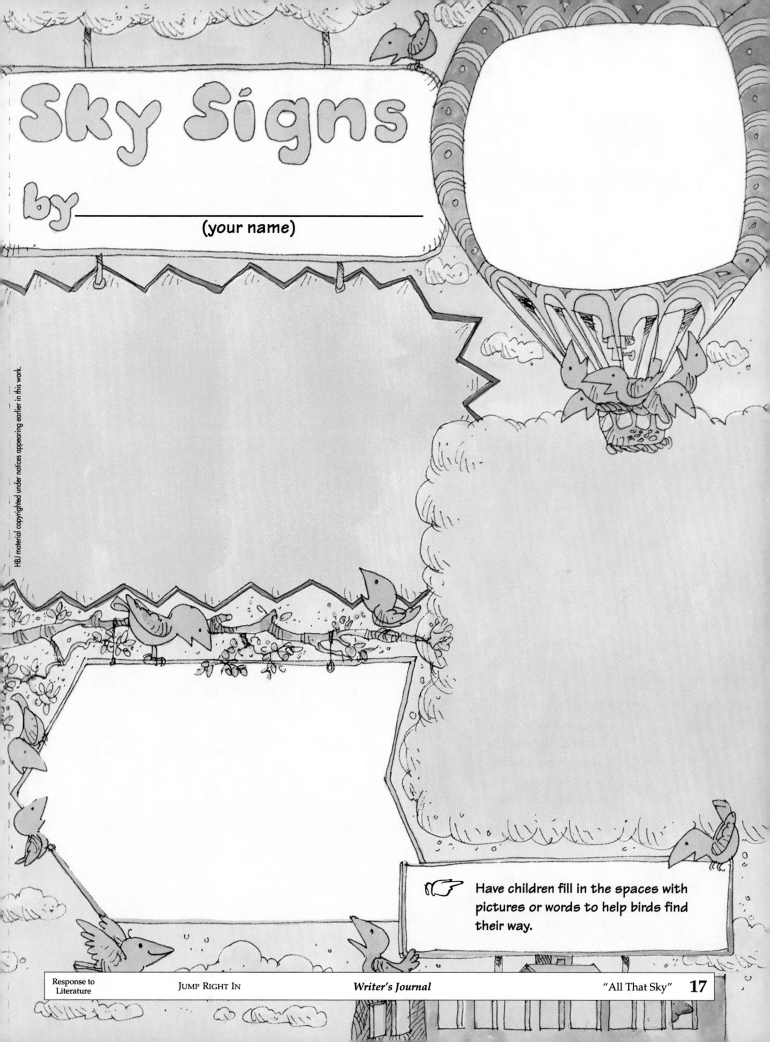

Sky Signs

by _____
(your name)

Have children fill in the spaces with pictures or words to help birds find their way.

QUACK
A Ducky Letter

Dear Mother Duck,

Have children pretend to be a little duck from the story. Have them write a letter telling Mother Duck where they went.

 Love and quacks,

_____
(your name) as Little Duck

"Me Too!" said ....
(your name)

Have children draw themselves doing something they would like to do in the first box. Have them write about it.

What **W**ill **H**appen?

What will this be?

What will come from the egg?

Peep, peep

☞ Have children look at the pictures, then answer the questions by drawing in the spaces and writing their answers.

Knows

_____ (your name)

What will the bird do?

What will the ducks do?

HBJ material copyrighted under notices appearing earlier in this work.

Let Me Out!

by _____
(your name)

☞ Have children draw themselves in the egg with the baby chick. Have them draw how they will get out. Tell children to write the sounds they would make while getting out.

Bet _____ Can Lift It!

This is how!

☞ Have children draw their facial features on the image and fill the basket with objects they think would make it hard to lift. Then ask them to write inside the speech balloon their ideas about how to lift the basket .

TEAR IT OUT

by _____

(your name)

☞ Have children make a book about things they'd like to try. Encourage them to make up their own title or use the title "Things I'd Like to Try." Have them decorate the front cover and complete the remaining pages.

Things _____ Would Like to Try in the Water
(your name)

Writer's Journal

Things _____
(Your Name)

Would Like to Try in the Sky

Things _____ (your name) _____ Would Like to Try on a Farm

Writer's Journal

Things _____
Would Like to Try at a Circus

Things _____
(your name)
Would Like to Try at Home

COLOR
THE
SKY

CONTENTS

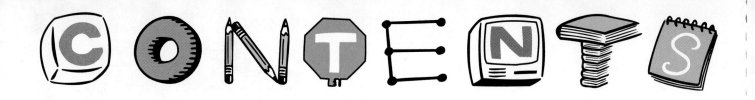

(Your Name)

and a Friend Get Together

Have children draw their facial features on the image. Have them write what they might say to make friends with another child.

What _____ and a Friend
(your name)
Can Play

Have children draw themselves playing with a friend in an imaginative way. Have them write about their picture either here or on another sheet of paper.

_____ 's Musical Instrument
(your name)

☞ Ask children to draw a musical instrument that two friends can play together at the same time. Then have children name their instrument.

's Rule

_____
(your name)

☞ Have children imagine they are babysitting for the monkeys in the story. Ask them to make up a rule of behavior for the monkeys. They can draw and write their rule.

_____
(your name)

Where are they going?

Tell how you know.

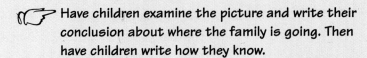 Have children examine the picture and write their conclusion about where the family is going. Then have children write how they know.

Finds the Clues

What will they do there?

Tell how you know.

☞ Have children write their conclusions about what the family will do while camping. Have them write how they know. Have them circle the clues that led them to their conclusions.

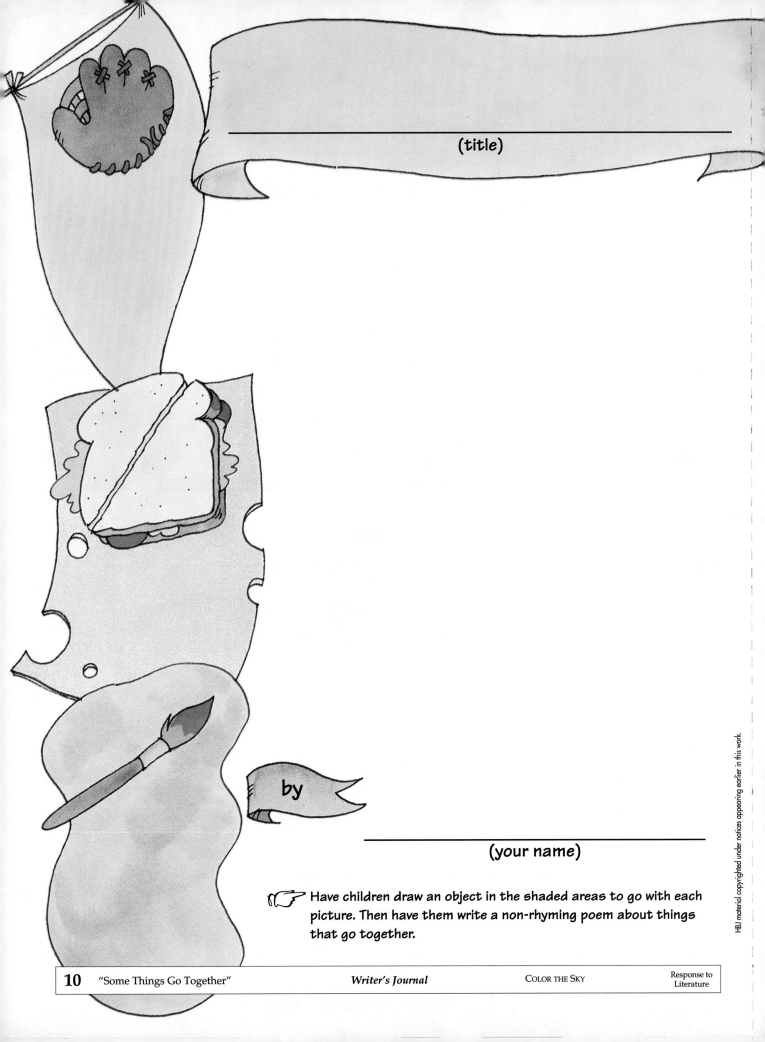

_____
(title)

by

_____
(your name)

☞ Have children draw an object in the shaded areas to go with each
picture. Then have them write a non-rhyming poem about things
that go together.

_____
(your name)

's Animal Family

Have children draw a baby animal and its parents. Have them write about their picture.

(YOUR NAME)

Names the Animals

Baby

Have children name each animal. Have them write about one
of the animal's features that helped them think of a name.

Friends Like Us

Turn to page 14.

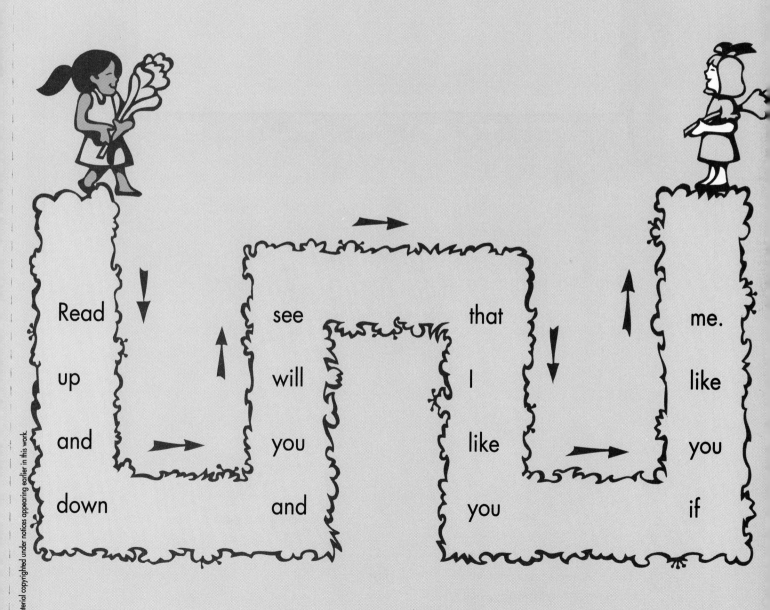

Read up and down

see will you and

that I like you

me. like you if

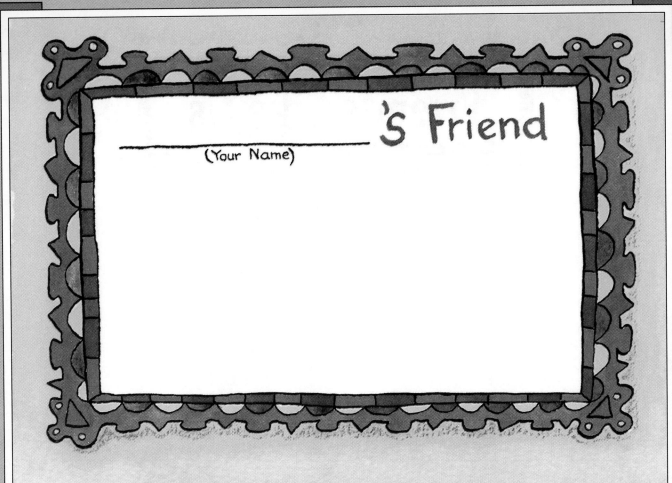

_____'s Friend
(Your Name)

☞ Have children draw a picture of a friend. Have them write why they like their friend.

_____'S
(your name)

BEST FRIEND

Have children draw a picture of a special thing their best friend or another child they know can do. Then have them write about their picture.

WHAT _____
AND A FRIEND CAN DO

Have children draw themselves and a friend doing something they can really do. Then have them write about their drawing.

WHAT _____
(your name)
AND A FRIEND
CAN'T DO

☞ Have children draw themselves and the same friend, doing something make-believe that they really can't do. Then have them write about it.

Bear Talks to _____

Have children write what Bear would say about why he likes to ride a bike slowly.

Mouse Talks To _____
(your name)

☞ Have children write what Mouse would say about why he likes to ride a bike fast.

_____
(your name)

baseball

playhouse

seesaw

football

👉 Have children draw themselves on the playground. Have them write what they would like to play with. Encourage children to try to use two compound words.

Dear Porcupine,

Your friend,

_____
(your name)

Have children write a letter to the porcupine telling why they are glad to be its friend.

Welcome to _____'s Classroom
(your name)

**Things Very Tall
Mouse Sees**

**Things Very Short
Mouse Sees**

👉 Tell children to imagine that Very Tall Mouse and Very Short
Mouse are visiting the classroom. Have them draw the things
each mouse might notice. Have children write what they
would tell the mice about their classroom.

_____'s Sandwich

(your name)

☞ Have children draw a favorite sandwich they can make themselves. Have them write directions telling how to make the sandwich. Encourage them to number their directions.

TEAR IT OUT

_____'s Dream Vacation

(your name)

⊖ Photo Album ⊖

☞ Have children imagine that they are going on a dream vacation.
Have them decorate the cover of their photo album.

_____'s
(your name)

Trip to the Fair

Have children draw themselves on their favorite ride. Have them write a caption to go with their picture.

Writer's Journal

_____
(your name)

's Trip to a Castle

Have children draw themselves and a friend or two story characters in the castle. Have them write a caption to go with their picture.

's **Trip to the Mountains**

_____
(your name)

Have children draw themselves in the snow scene.
Have them write a caption to go with their picture.

_____'s Trip to the Beach
(your name)

 Have children draw themselves in the beach scene.
Have them write a caption to go with their picture.

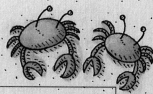

_____'s
(your name)
Trip to Outer Space

Have children draw themselves and a friend or a story character in the spaceship. Have them write a caption to go with the picture.

WRITER'S HANDBOOK

This is your Writer's Handbook. It will help you check your own writing.

Every sentence ends with an end mark.

Use a **period** at the end of a sentence that tells something.

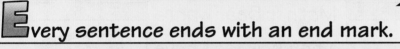

The two frogs met at the top of the hill**.**

Use a **question mark** at the end of a sentence that asks something.

Where are you going**?**

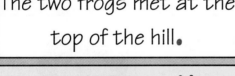

Use an **exclamation point** at the end of a sentence that shows strong feeling.

How smart you are**!**

CAPITAL LETTERS

Is this fish too little? It looks good to me.

Begin the **first word of a sentence** with a capital letter.

Write the **word I** as a capital letter.

Mother Bear wants a fish now, so I have to catch one.

ME!

Grampy gave Punky a little fishing pole.

Begin the **name of a person** with a capital letter.

Begin the **title of a person** with a capital letter. These are titles:

Mr. Mrs.
Ms. Miss
Dr.

"Only four?" asked Mrs. Brown.

Other Capital Letters

Begin the **name of a pet** with a capital letter.

> The farmer's dog, **Mack**, ate the cake.

Animal Names

Begin the **name of a day of the week** with a capital letter.

> Did Lionel eat vegetables on **Saturday?**

Begin the **name of a month** with a capital letter.

> Did Arthur and D.W. go to the beach in **July?**

Begin each important word in the **title of a story** with a capital letter.

> One of the stories about Frog and Toad is **"Cookies." "Sea Frog, City Frog"** is a funny story.

Titles

EDITOR'S MARKS

You can use these marks when you revise and proofread your own writing.

≡   **Make this a capital letter.**

⊙   **Add a period.**

?   **Add a question mark.**

!   **Add an exclamation point.**

Do you like to go fishing? I do! i like to sit in the boat. i like to watch the water and the sky Sometimes i like to feel the waves, too i don't really care about catching fish. but I love to go fishing!

WRITER'S HANDBOOK

This is your Writer's Handbook. It will help you check your own writing.

END MARKS

Every sentence ends with an end mark.

Use a **period** at the end of a sentence that tells about someone.

I went walking.

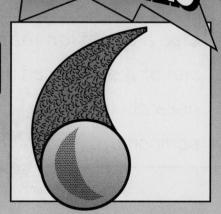

Use a **period** at the end of a sentence that tells about something.

Walking fast is fun.

MORE END MARKS

Use a **question mark** at the end of a sentence that asks about something.

What did you see?

Use a **question mark** at the end of a sentence that asks about someone.

Did you go walking?

Use an **exclamation point** at the end of a sentence that shows strong feeling.

I saw a lot of animals following me!

CAPITAL LETTERS

Begin the **first word** of a sentence with a capital letter.

On the way she met a sheep.

How did Silly Sally get to town?

Write the word **I** as a capital letter.

ME!

And **I** learned to love from a friend like you.

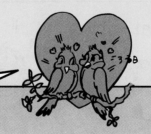

MORE CAPITAL LETTERS

Begin the **name** of a person with a capital letter.

She tickled **Neddy Buttercup.**

People

Begin the **title of a person** with a capital letter. These are titles: Mr. Mrs. Ms. Miss Dr.

Did **Miss** Day see all those animals?

Titles of a Person

Begin the **name of a pet** with a capital letter.

Did your dog **Tag** follow you?

Animal Names

MORE CAPITAL LETTERS

Begin the **name of a day of the week** with a capital letter.

Were you as nice as a bunny on **Monday**?

Begin the **name of a month** with a capital letter.

Were you as busy as a bee in **April**?

Begin each important word in the **title of a story** with a capital letter.

First we read "**Quick as a Cricket**." Then we read "**My Friends**."

EDITOR'S MARKS

You can use these marks when you revise and proofread your own writing.

≡   Make this a capital letter.
⊙   Add a period.
?   Add a question mark.
!   Add an exclamation point.

I have lots of pets⊙ Would you like to meet them? This is my little dog toby. this is my big cat cal. can you hear my birds singing? They are called chip and chap. i have some fish, too. I love all my pets!